FARM MACHINERY

HEAVY EQUIPMENT

David and Patricia Armentrout

The Rourke Book Co., Inc.
Vero Beach, Florida 32964

PHOTO CREDITS
© John Deere: title page and pages 4, 8, 10; © CASE: pages 7,
13, 15, 17, 18, 21; © Courtesy of Kubota Corporation: page 12; ©
Dave Rogers: cover

ACKNOWLEDGEMENTS
The authors thank Dave Rogers for his help in the preparation of
this book.

Library of Congress Cataloging-in-Publication Data

Armentrout, Patricia, 1960-
   Farm machinery / by Patricia Armentrout and David Armentrout.
     p. cm. — (Heavy Equipment)
   Includes index.
   ISBN 1-55916-135-3
   1. Agricultural machinery—Juvenile literature.   [1. Agricultural
Machinery. 2. Machinery.]
I. Armentrout, David, 1962- . II. Title.   III. Series: Armentrout,
Patricia, 1960- Heavy Equipment.
S675.25.A46 1995
631.3' 7—dc20   95–3977
                                       CIP
                                       AC

Printed in the USA

TABLE OF CONTENTS

PLANTING CROPS

Hundreds of years ago, men and women who planted crops used simple tools like sticks and deer antlers to loosen and **cultivate** (KUL tuh VATE) the soil. Cultivating the soil is a process of preparing the earth for planting crops.

Today's tools are pieces of heavy equipment that make the job of planting crops faster and easier.

Tractors pull planting attachments through crop fields

THE FIRST PLOW

The first plow was made of wooden beams with a wooden wedge that cut through the soil. Handles attached to the beams made it possible for farmers to push the plow.

The wooden plow could not cut through hard soil and sod. Work animals were then used to move the plow. Wheels were attached to ease movement. Eventually new plows were invented that used metal cutting blades to turn over, or till, the soil.

This plow attachment has metal disc blades that cut through hard soil

TRACTORS

The tractor is the most important piece of farm equipment. With front and rear attachments, the tractor is used to plow, cultivate, rake, plant, fertilize, and even mow.

The farm tractor needs to be very powerful. **Turbine** (TER bine) engines provide power for the tractor. Large rubber-tired wheels move it across the land.

Large turbine tractors can plow almost a hundred acres of land in an eight-hour workday.

A crop farm like this one uses many pieces of machinery

THE HARVESTER

A harvester is a machine that is used to **harvest** (HAR vest), or pick, crops.

The first harvesters were called reapers. The reaper was used to harvest grains like wheat, barley, and oats. Revolving bars of teeth pushed the grains against a cutting blade. After the reaper cut the grain, a reel put the grain on a **conveyor** (kun VAY or), or moving belt, and farm workers would tie the grain in bundles.

Over the years the reaper was developed into a more efficient machine called the combine.

A combine moves through the field in rows as it harvests corn

Modern tractors are built for comfort with the controls right at the operator's fingertips

Dried hay is collected and rolled into round bales

THE COMBINE

The combine, a harvesting machine, can be found on almost any large crop farm. Its main purpose is to cut and thresh grain. Threshing is a process of separating the grain from the stalk.

Early combines used in the 1920's had separate motors and were pulled by tractors. Today combines are large **self-propelled** (SELF-pro PELD) machines.

With the use of many attachments, a combine can go from harvesting late summer corn to harvesting rice, soybeans, or winter wheat.

Harvested grain is emptied from the combine into a bin for easy removal from the field

HARVESTING HAY

The **windrower** (WIN dro er) is a hay-cutting machine. It travels slowly, less than 10 miles an hour, but cuts hay at 1,500 strokes a minute!

The purpose of the windrower is to cut fields of hay and leave it in rows to dry. The hot sun dries the hay. The hay is then baled, or packed in a bundle, and stored in barns.

The windrower is also used to harvest other crops like green peas, grass seed, and alfalfa.

This windrower can be used to cut hay or harvest crops like green beans or alfalfa

COTTON HARVESTING MACHINES

At harvest time, a cotton stripper is driven through the fields removing the cotton **bolls** (bolz). A spindle harvester, another cotton picking machine, gathers and winds only the cotton lint from the bolls.

A cotton gin, a machine that removes the seeds from the lint, used to be located on every plantation, or farm. Today the harvested cotton is trucked to large factories.

Modern machines wash and dry the lint. The clean lint is sent through a gin where revolving teeth pull the lint, leaving the seed behind.

Harvested cotton is loaded up, ready to be trucked to the factory

PEOPLE WHO WORK ON FARMS

Farm workers are responsible for plowing, planting, and harvesting crops. They are the ones seen driving the tractors and combines through fields. Other workers drive large dump trucks. They wait in the field until the combine driver empties the load. The truck driver then takes the harvest to be stored or processed.

But what happens when a tractor or combine breaks down? Some farms have live-in mechanics. They are available 24 hours a day to repair farm equipment.

Farm mechanics can do a range of repair and maintaince work on tractors

TODAY'S FARMS

Over the years, U.S. farms have changed. The farm fields have grown in size. The field sizes have grown to make room for big machines like combine harvesters and windrowers.

These big farm machines have made it possible to produce large food crops, such as wheat and corn, and fiber crops, like cotton.

The farm workers have had to change too. Today some farm workers learn a special job and travel from farm to farm. They plant, harvest, or repair equipment, doing whatever work is needed.

Glossary

bolls (bolz) — seed pods

conveyor (kun VAY or) — a moving belt surface where items are placed and transferred somewhere else

cultivate (KUL tuh VATE) — to prepare soil for raising crops

harvest (HAR vest) — gathering or picking crops

self-propelled (SELF-pro PELD) — self-moving

turbine (TER bine) — a type of powerful engine or machine that get its power by water pressure, gas, or steam

windrower (WIN dro er) — a machine used to harvest hay

INDEX